THE NIOBE POEMS

the thing I came for:
the wreck and not the story of the wreck
the thing itself and not the myth
                              —Adrienne Rich

Kate
Daniels

*The Niobe
Poems*

University of Pittsburgh Press

Published by the University of Pittsburgh Press, Pittsburgh, Pa. 15260
Copyright © 1988, Kate Daniels
All rights reserved
Feffer and Simons, Inc., London
Manufactured in the United States of America

Library of Congress Cataloging in Publication Data
Daniels, Kate, 1953–
  The Niobe poems.
  (Pitt poetry series)
  I. Title.   II. Series.
  PS3554.A5636N56   1988   811'.54   88-4754
  ISBN 0-8229-3596-1
  ISBN 0-8229-5411-7 (pbk.)

The author and publisher wish to express their grateful acknowledgment to
the following publications in which some of these poems first appeared: *Iron-
wood* ("After Pain Passes" and "Tenderness"); *The Massachusetts Review*
("Bus Ride" and "War Photo"); and *New England Review and Bread Loaf
Quarterly* ("After the Funeral," "Bathing," "Before the Funeral," "Family
Life," "Final Visit," "The Gods Are Optional," "Lying Down," and "Ménage
à trois").

The poem which appears on page xv is copyrighted © 1961 by David Ignatow.
Reprinted from David Ignatow, *Poems, 1934–1969* by permission of Wesleyan
University Press.

*The publication of this book is supported by grants
from the National Endowment for the Arts
in Washington, D.C., a Federal agency,
and the Pennsylvania Council on the Arts.*

This book is for my friends
at the Bunting Institute—
who showed me the way
of the new Niobe—
*changed from a myth
to a woman at last* . . .

Contents

Contents

THE MYTH OF NIOBE

The mortal Niobe was the happiest and proudest of mothers. When she presumed to declare her happiness and her pride greater than that of Leto, the goddess took offense and asked her own children to punish Niobe for her arrogance. Apollo and Artemis used their silver arrows to take the lives of Niobe's fourteen children, her seven sons and seven daughters. Sick with despair, Niobe fled to the wilderness where she was turned into a rock. From the rock flowed a continual stream of water formed by the grieving mother's tears.

HOW THE MYTH WAS HANDED DOWN

Ovid tells the most detailed story of Niobe in Book Six of the *Metamorphoses*. Niobe, the daughter of Tantalus and the wife of Amphion, king of Thebes, was the mother of fourteen children: seven sons and seven daughters. Proud, arrogant, and irreverent like her father, she made the fatal mistake of boasting of the superiority of her children to those of the goddess Leto who had borne only two: the divine twins, Apollo and Artemis. Outraged at Niobe's presumptuousness, Leto determined to punish her. At their mother's bidding, Artemis and Apollo murdered all fourteen of the Niobids, not sparing even one, in spite of the mortal mother's plea to save her last and littlest daughter. Apollo shot the seven boys as they played and exercised on a field outside town. Artemis took the lives of the seven girls as they bent over the dead bodies of their brothers and of their father, who had taken his own life, overwhelmed by grief at the loss of his sons. Niobe sat among the many bodies, utterly crushed:

> So she sat there,
> A childless woman among her sons, her daughters,
> Beside her husband, and never moved; no air
> Lifted her hair, the color of her features
> Was waxen, and her eyes were fixed and staring,
> The picture of utter grief, and in the picture
> No sign of life at all: the tongue was frozen
> To the roof of the mouth; no pulse beat in the veins;
> Neck could not bend, nor arms be moved, nor feet
> Go back or forward; and the vitals hardened
> To rock, but still she weeps; and she is carried,
> Caught up in a whirlwind, to her native mountains,
> Where, on a summit, a queen deposed, she rests,
> Still weeping: even to this day the marble
> Trickles with tears.

Homer tells a slightly different story in Book XXIV of *The Iliad*:

We are told
that even Niobe in her extremity
took thought for bread—though all her brood had perished,
her six young girls and six tall sons, Apollo,
making his silver longbow whip and sing
shot the lads down, and Artemis with raining
arrows killed the daughters—all this after
Niobe had compared herself with Leto,
the smooth-cheeked goddess.
                              She had borne two children,
Niobe said, How many have I borne!
But soon those two destroyed the twelve.
                              Besides
nine days the dead lay stark, no one could bury them,
for Zeus had turned all folks of theirs to stone.
The gods made graves for them on the tenth day,
and then at last, being weak and spent with weeping,
Niobe thought of food. Among the rocks
of Sipylos' lonely mountainside, where nymphs
who race Akheloios river go to rest,
she, too, long turned to stone, somewhere broods on
the gall immortal gods gave her to drink.

Dante mentions Niobe in Canto XII of the *Purgatorio* where she is in company with those who have suffered the "vice of Pride, the Haughty who have been brought low." "O Niobe, with sorrowing eyes I saw thy slaughtered children, seven on either side, and thee atween."

Edith Hamilton: "Insolent words uttered in the arrogant consciousness of power were always heard in heaven and always punished."

Robert Graves: "All men mourned for Amphion, declaring the extinction of his race, but none mourned Niobe."

The Woman's Encyclopedia of Myths and Secrets: "Niobe: 'Snowy One,' Anatolian Mountain-goddesss whose worshippers were destroyed by patriarchal Hellenistic tribes. Greek myth therefore made her a mother forever mourning her 'children' slain by the Olympian gods. Greek writers pretended she was a woman too proud of her children, so the gods killed them to punish her hubris."

DRAMATIS PERSONAE

NIOBE: the mortal mother of fourteen, seven sons and seven daughters, who inherited the fatal arrogance of her father, Tantalus, who had offended the gods, thus incurring his own eternal punishment and the ongoing misfortune of his descendants.

LETO: the goddess daughter of the Titans Phoebe and Coeus. She bore twins to Zeus, Apollo and Artemis.

ARTEMIS: the divine huntress, goddess of the moon, and the Lady of Wild Things. As Diana, goddess of the hunt, she protected and nurtured young life like all good hunters, but she was also capable of swift and vengeful action.

APOLLO: the archer god, the god of light, the god of truth, often called the most Greek of all the gods. His silver bow was usually drawn for beneficent purposes; nevertheless, he, like his twin sister Artemis, could be merciless and cruel.

THE NIOBIDS: the children of Niobe.

AMPHION: the husband of Niobe who took his own life in despair after the deaths of his seven sons. As a youth, Amphion had been a superb musician. Building a wall around Thebes, he made such beautiful music on his lyre that the stones moved themselves into place.

THE PHOENIX: the mythological bird of the sun that lived for a thousand years. When the time of its death approached, the Phoenix prepared itself a fragrant nest to use as a funeral pyre. Inside this nest, it set itself afire, only to rise again from one spark in the ashes to live through another cycle of centuries.

NIOBE SPEAKS
AS AN ABYSSINIAN WOMAN

"How can a man know what a woman's life is? The man spends a night by a woman and goes away. His life and body are always the same. The woman conceives. As a mother she is another person from the woman without child. She carries the fruit of the night nine months long in her body. Something grows. Something grows into her life that never again departs from it. She is a mother. She is and remains a mother even though her child die, even though all her children die. For at one time she carried the child under her heart. And it does not go out of her heart ever again. Not even when it is dead."

—from *Essays on a Science of Mythology*

A NIOBE POEM
BY DAVID IGNATOW

Mother and Child

She feared the baby would fall,
Upside down she held it.
She loved her child.
As a born baby, it was a practical thing,
handled by doctors. As a drowned baby,
it still would exist.

By accident it died inside its tub.
She carried it carefully to its crib
and there rocked it, as she called for help.
Help, help, she called.
Help, help, she whispered,
hands resting upon her.

THE GODS / THE MYTH
THE ACCIDENT

The Little King

He rode to bed that last night
on a throne of arms,
the seat of his pants
sticky with pine tar,
an overgrown zucchini
standing in for a sceptre.

Were the gods watching
even then? Were they saying,
that's him, that's the one
we want, the one
we get to have
because we're strong enough
to take him,
because we do not care
about the mortal mother
he'll leave behind,
her wailing, her wild
weeping, the pills
she'll have to take to sleep,
her strong and suffocating wish
to throw herself after him
into the earth, as if he were a god
himself, who had punished her
by taking away all she lived for,
every single thing she loved.

The Gods Are Optional

The gods sat in the trees
that evening, green and darkening,
lingering over a last coffee,
coffee with a shot of rum.
The river was talking to them
but they were gods and didn't have
to listen. Even in the trees
it was hot that night. The leaves were not
delightful as they knew how to be.
The gods stirred in the trees, they looked
away. The river was talking
to them more urgently. "I don't
want this," it said. "I don't need it."
But the gods had worked enough
that day. And the evening
was so hot the little mortal
flung himself into the water.

Inside the house beside the river,
someone talked on the telephone.
Someone wrote in a notebook.
The windows were just openings
no one happened to look through.
The hands on the clock lurched forward forever.

Afterwards Apollo

Walked around in the dark woods,
shaking his head, his bow loose
in his nervous hand.
He wasn't sure what had happened,
why there had been all that blood
and the piteous wailing.
And why it had been
his job, anyway,
to murder children.

If you could have seen him then
illuminated from within
by the force of his thinking
like an ancient tree ignited
for a moment by a lightning bolt,
would he have seemed magnanimous, ·
as in the legend, or only humanly
confused? The huge wooden branches
groaning and glistening with light
in the dark. The two feelings
fighting in him, and not
being able to tell, ever,
which one would win.

But Artemis

Was less uncertain than her brother.
She lay down in her favorite wood
and licked her privates and watched
the night grow darker. She could hear
Apollo pacing through the woods,
working it out. She laughed
a low, contented laugh and threaded
her fingers through her pubic hair.
She needed this every now and then.
She liked it
when they recognized her fatal form
and understood her hunter's task.
The screams only wakened something
harder and more
untouchable in her. And *then*
it really was almost
sexual: great, winglike fans
rising inside, a low fire
in her groin, her nipples standing out
taut and black.

She was never sorry afterwards,
or tortured by ambiguity.
There was a reason somewhere
but that was not
her job. Because she
was a god.
She laughed, watching
them rage at her,
at the way they couldn't stop
hating her. Didn't they know
after all this time?
Didn't they see

there was nothing
any of them could do to her.
She kept on floating above them,
lovely and terrible,
but still somehow
desirable.

The Death of the Niobids

Afterwards it was very still.
For a short while
they lay there alone
and no one knew
what had happened.
The sun beat down
on the broken bodies.
The silver arrows glittered
in the summer light.

If you had come upon it
would you have believed
what you saw? The country
at peace but the family
slaughtered at the municipal park.

Would you have shaken your head
and hurried on, disbelieving?
Or would you have been the one
who went on to the palace
after covering the bodies,
the one who had to tell Niobe,
who placed his hands on her shoulders
that were turned to glass
and forced her down into a chair
and brought the sip of water.
Were you the one, then,
who told her to submit
and advised her to accept
whatever the gods dished out?

Then it was you
she came to afterwards,
standing in your preacher's frock.
After the funeral.
After the mourning.
After the rock.
You were the one
she looked in the face
and told to fuck off.

BEFORE THE ACCIDENT /
A FAMILY ROMANCE

Tenderness

Being afraid of men
she has made one
hoping it would help.
But when it was time
her fear was too great
to push him out.
Men in masks
and bright glasses
cut him free,
held him up for a moment
in the sanctifying light
so she could see
his genitals,
purple and engorged,
the small promise they made.

What she was imagining
was the future,
not his greatness or ambition
or the height he would attain,
but all the women
he could enter and destroy
and also those
who would teach him to be tender.

Jeunes mères

Niobe's friend Brenda
is a housewife
at home, alone, with her baby.
She is giving milk
most of the time, making milk
the rest. Her body
is too tired
to heat itself.
All day long
she wears her robe,
shuts the windows and doors
on the Florida spring
and nurses the baby
and makes the milk:
the fresh milk coolly
spurting from her breasts,
the old milk, sour,
on the baby and the blankets.

When Niobe visits with her baby,
she peers in through a darkened window.
She waits at a blank, locked door.
Inside, she sees the place where Brenda
has been nursing, the rags
and pillows all around her chair.
The remote control to the TV
next to her hand.
Now she is trapped in there
with Brenda and the heat
and the sound of babies sucking milk.
The men have abandoned them
for the entire day.
They are alone in there

but together, bursting with blood and milk.
There is a sweet smell of fruit
in a bowl, uneaten and rotting.
They sit across from each other
on the bed, afraid to say anything.

Perfect

Niobe knows some children
can't be trusted with toys.
They cut the hair,
burn in half the plastic soldiers,
take apart, rip up, destroy
what was intended for their pleasure.
And when the wounded things
are lying damaged on the floor, she wonders
if they want them whole again:
a perfect world where what is done
is undone in order to take place again,
desire destroying the perfect image
in any small occurrence:
the baseball shattering the plate glass window,
the pebble hemorrhaging the muddy puddle.

The look on the face of the child
smashing her toys apart announces
she wants more than this,
the smug forms the world assumes
beneath our eyes and hands.
Underneath, something different rumbles
through the troubled insides of those like her.
The graffitied cities are a sign.
All the broken marriages.
What rages, trapped, within our little bodies?

Child Abuse

Niobe can't read
but she doesn't need anything
from books. She's a farm wife
with seven children and an ailing man.
She works all day.
At night, she prays and sews and sleeps.

Her girl Lucille
is twelve this summer.
Under the apple trees
she reads from a green-backed book.
Niobe, beating biscuits at the iron stove,
watches through the open window.
She loves her daughter.
She knows she does.

But the row of books
in the pastor's parlor
is torturous to her: the worlds
of words and pictures
where she can never go.
But 'Cille is there
right now, dancing
on a flowered carpet, or maybe
she is walking in a garden
or simply sitting softly
on a yellow satin sofa.

Without a word, Niobe
goes outside and strips a switch
from the cherry tree and beats
her daughter's legs until they bleed.

Thief

"He was not mine,
the child I held,
newborn and helpless.
I remember his smell,
small and milky,
and my hand holding
his feet together.
Soft Scarlatti in the background,
the rush of traffic in the street,
and rain falling blankly
as an omniscient narrator
in a complicated novel.
Compulsively, I opened my blouse
and pushed his mouth
toward my breast.
When he took it,
a new sound was struck
from my throat.
For a moment, I gloried
in the hard circle,
the fast wetness,
the small warm hole
of moving mouth.
Thirty seconds or so
he sucked,
then pulled back
with all his tiny strength
and screamed at me
when nothing spewed forth
but my own bad need.

My red nipple glistened
with spittle, empty
of milk. It jutted
into the quiet room
like a finger, accusing and excited.
It glowed in the lamplight,
exclaiming my theft."

Ménage à trois

Niobe keeps thinking of his eyes
inside her, before he was born. How large
they are, how brown. How their shape
is the shape of her eyes, and her mother's,
and others, far back, she never knew.
Niobe wonders what it felt like
to open them in there, the thick
and fecund liquid pressing all over.
The slow and downward drag
of those long lashes
and what it was he saw
inside her that he'll never tell,
that even his father will never know.
                                    And that

is what really thrills Niobe:
how different it is
between the father
and the son. How much
more intimate with the son.
And how this is the father's
greatest fear.

Family Life

All evening, the man sits in the chair,
pretending he's reading, head down, hunched
against the child's cries, the woman's body
that is not the same since the child passed through.

Surely he is thinking of the gods,
the purity and clarity of their lives,
something like the saints'
but without the suffering.

He is considering the precision
of wrath and vengeance, justice
and retribution, of terror's clean edge
whetted with logic.

Up there on the mountain
it must be simple to see
a mortal man's life
break down to this:

an upstairs flat of secondhand furniture
where the child is shrieking
and the woman is exhausted
from nursing all day.

Of course, he could go out.
But the men at the bar
are just like him, aren't they?
Stunned and unhappy, unsure

what happened. It's impossible
to imagine how the gods live, anyway.
Untouched, I guess. So high
no one can see them.
And they can barely hear us,
how much we need them,
how much we hate them
for their silence and their distance.

Fragile

After the quarrel
the house quivers.
The cutlery flashes
on the hard wood table.
The windows speak back.
It is very hard to walk
quietly now. The bodies
are so loud and so terribly
sorry. But they have gone
too far to come back home.
Like swimmers taken out
by an uncharted current
they're on their way
to disaster.
All they can hope
is to wash up
fragile as a shell
on another shore,
afraid of everything
they used to love:
the air, the sun,
the unknown human hand
coming down from above.

Amphion and the New Gnostics

Lying together in the long evenings
after love was the culmination
of all he wanted, all he'd been led
to desire and believe: the shadows softening
her beautiful body, the narcotic
odor of female love.
Her dark eyes were fastened
like an animal's on him.
                            Years passed
until he bemoaned familiarity,
the predictable movements her body made.
Now, after love, she still watched him,
but from a distance, wondering
which way he would go:
with the rest of the men
to plunder the secrets
from another woman's body?
Or with the few new gnostics
who went to women like going to school,
traced the wrinkles growing
like evolving maps, fondled the soft fall
of childbearing belly, opened themselves
to the other like a book
and understood the hard work
it took to make a love.

Her Body

They are fighting over it again:
too big here, too little there.
The girls in the magazines
make it look so easy
to be a goddess, and that's
what he deserves: a woman who knows
the worth of a man and wouldn't dare
disparage his lopsided testicles
or his thinning hair.

So they're fighting: he's demanding,
she's resisting, though she doesn't hold
his fear against him. She cherishes
the secret he can't quite bear:
her fallen ass he loves so much
that he whimpers to get behind it,
to plow into her, to crow and bark
like a mindless animal, to take her,
to take her, to take her willing body
to the end of the road.

Bathing

He always bathed afterwards,
slipping his fine and sticky
genitals over the cool rim
of the porcelain sink.
She lay in the other room,
smoking and staring tiredly
out the window. The tiny sounds
of the suds came to her
worrisomely. The *suck-suck*
sounds of his hand lathering
soap into his tight, dark curls.
Then the farewell groan of the drain.
The energetic flap of the towel.
When he was before her again,
his teeth covered by a smile,
the sweat and stench removed,
she studied him from the crushed
bed, admiring his cruel
beauty, her body still marked
and odorous. His, clean
and unstained, amnesiac
already.

Precious

Afterwards, he holds himself
in his two hands, moist
and weighty, eyes closed, breath
almost absent,
going away somewhere
by himself: a whole room
of blue air, empty
and undemanding.

But now Niobe wants
to be held, still
quivering and wet.
To lie there together
in the aftershock of love
and marvel at being
not gods anymore:
small and irreducible,
survivors in the ruins
of a blown-up building.

Narcissus, on his way to die,
leaned over the boat
to find his face in the fading water,
adoring himself a final time.
And the man Niobe married and loved
lies as if alone
on the bed they share, caressing
his cock with his marvelous hands.
Shouldn't she know
he will be no help
when the tragedy comes?
Can't she see whose image he seeks

in her transformed face?
What is she beneath him?
Whose sounds are those?
And how can he hear her
at all, so taken is he
with his own delight?

AFTER THE ACCIDENT /
THE FUNERAL

After Pain Passes

It's like being young again
before complexity was an issue
or a concept. It's like waking up
in the middle of a bad situation—
the lover you're leaving is sleeping there
but for a moment you forget.
For a moment, it is only dark and the body
beside you is one you want.
For a moment, there's pure clarity
and divisions like opening an orange
with your hands instead of a knife.
The clean way the skin leaves the body.
The sharp smell.
That one moment you focus
on the ripped whiteness
fallen to the side and forget
the fruit, everything you've known it to be.

The Bedspread

"A hundred times I have made this bed,
smoothed the tufted white cotton
over the colorful sheets, tucked
a thick fold under the lumpy pillow.
And more often I have lain here
with a small child, his yellow hair
spilling over both of us, silliness
filling the bedroom air.

The night they pulled him from the river,
his grandfather fetched this heavy spread
to wrap the little body in. Steadily,
he walked down the long wood hall,
and pulled it from the bed,
and carried it down to the bright backyard,
and laid it out among the divers and the lights.

I can understand how a child falls in the river,
how water takes the breath away:
a careless game on the slippery bulkhead,
the false courage of a five-year-old.
What I can't understand
is that long walk down the empty hallway
past the mother in the wooden chair,
her hands at her face, the precise steadiness
of the footfalls from room to room,
or the silence of the walker,
the determination and the dry face,
the unrivalled tenderness of that final act.
I don't understand how he stood upright,
how he even moved or breathed,
or how his hands made the motions
unmaking the bed where no one would ever sleep again."

Final Visit

It was only a small sound,
round but broken,
cut off and quiet.
A sound pouring out
before she could stop it.
It entered the room
where the yellow-haired child
reposed among flowers.

From the other parlor
we heard it all: the sorrow
and the terrible love.
Among the roses' odor
there was horror
and guilt.

It was only a small sound,
round and barely spoken,
a final exchange
between mother and son.
Now the sound goes round
in a cave of sorrow.
She lives there alone,
small and broken.

The Poem

Niobe had just lost her son.
To help herself, she read a poem
to those assembled in the funeral home,
a poem about pain and mercy and mother love.
When it was over, she refolded the paper
along its newly creased lines,
slid it back in the pocket
of the blue jacket in the coffin.

Her hands busy folding and tucking,
her mind wandered back to six months before,
buying the jacket at a large store
in a shopping mall. A couple of sizes
too big, so he could grow into it.
That was mercy: the price
and the purchase. The rest of it
and most of it was pain:
the creased lines of the poem
in that small blue pocket
and how quickly everything would turn to dust.

"I Was Afraid of Him"

"When I put the poem
in his jacket pocket
I was afraid of him
and his new secret.
He lay there dead
and calm, his eyes closed,
his head propped up
on a satin pillow.

He wouldn't say anything
back to us though we wailed
over him a day and a night,
wouldn't tell us why or how
the accident happened,
wouldn't explain the covered-up bruise
on the bridge of his nose.
So we smoothed his hair,
we touched his cheek
that was hard as metal.
We wept, we wept, we wept.

Now the world had lost
its usual shape: our little one
was large with a horrible knowledge
and we were small, diminished
by all we didn't know:
where he was and why it felt
so odd being there with him
not paying any attention to us
as if we were invisible,
as if we, ourselves,
were lying there dead.

The secret was unbearable.
It wasn't that we wanted him back.
No, no, we wanted to go
with him wherever he was,
to know the mysterious place
inside where he was living now
where children are large and parents
small, where no one speaks in voices
or opens their eyes, where it must be
lovely and magical, mustn't it?
to steal him away from us forever."

Lying Down

Nothing moves
in the house. A huge
silence, tense and quivering
as the hand of the masseuse
cupped barely above the body,
heat pouring down
in gentle sheets, the fine hairs
flickering up, underneath.

There is a smell of many flowers,
a heaviness of many shoes
still caked with mud
from the open grave.
They are lying down now
in separate rooms.
The scenes in their heads
keep stalling:
They see the diver surfacing
with the dripping body.
They see him weeping, alone,
at the end of the dock.
They see the diver, the body,
the weeping, the dock.

There is a cry from a darkened room
as utterly undone
as the guttural sounds
of giving birth.
But Niobe never hurt
this much giving birth
and nothing has prepared her
for the size of this.
She sees herself as never before:
the love she thought

so pure is sin:
she wants other boys dead
and her boy back.

Niobe lying on the bed
is so ugly with love,
nothing like a mother:
disfigured, untender.
But god keeps on going
at her. He opens
the door wider and bids them look.
He wants them to know
how hideous it is
where Niobe lives. How sentimental
and careless they've always been.
They've never seen anything
clearly. They've understood
nothing. He's god.
They're a bunch of dumb assholes.

Still Lying Down

At the blackboard, the professor
diagrams a math problem
that has no solution.
It's an equation that can't be solved.
A mystery of modern mathematics.

The little figures of the trapped numbers
are tipped over in his slanted script,
lithe, white bodies lost
in the black breadth
of the sprawling board.

You can almost imagine
they are lying down,
waiting for some genius
who might never come along,
to unlock them from themselves,

to solve the problem
and move them
at last
from this hell
on to the next one.

Before the Funeral

"I rubbed Niobe's legs
because the pills
had made them hurt.
We were all women
in her bedroom:
Niobe and her mother,
her best friend, and me.
At quarter to twelve
Niobe stood up
and put on the polka dot dress
that he had liked.
I slipped his toy
in my raincoat pocket.
Her best friend kept crying
and crying in her yellow hair.

Niobe paused, fastening the belt
on her blue silk dress.
Her eyes went away
out the window,
sunk into the river
where he had died.
And suddenly we were in church,
the colors warm and flooding,
the huge weight
of guilt bearing down.
Everyone could feel
Niobe not wanting
to live, not deserving
to die. Like a great mystery
she said to me, her hands warm
and shaking on my frozen cheeks,
I can't believe I'm alive
and burying my babychild."

After the Funeral

"I ate a sandwich
of ham and mustard
the maid brought me
from the dining room.
My husband was surrounded
by his boyhood friends,
dark and quiet
in business suits.
He couldn't eat.
After awhile,
we went upstairs.
I took a pill.
He took a pill.
We took off our shoes
and lay down beside each other
on the double bed.
First, we lay face to face.
Then we turned away.
We just lay there
awake, I think, no part
of our bodies touching. The pills
making our breathing
almost invisible, almost silent."

THE END OF THE STORY /
A NEW NARRATION /
A NEW NIOBE

The First Day of the Rest of Her Life

God was finally gone forever.
Niobe didn't fear him
anymore, didn't need him
for anything else.
She had disciplined herself
to handle the situation
and walked around now
coming back to life,
the memories of the children
flickering inside like snapshots
pasted in an album.

Occasionally, she could let herself
think about them, what it was like
when they were all together—
their funny songs, the different colors
of their hair, the yeasty smells
inside their hands when they were born.
But then she had to stop
before it went too far
and she remembered the end
of the story again.
She'd take a pill and go to sleep.

She knew she couldn't live for long
in that simmering moment
before a scream erupts.
The building-up feeling
is there, the horrible
hammering, and you know
if something drastic doesn't happen,
if someone doesn't help you,
the whole world will be shattered
by your fear and grief.

Niobe of the Painting

—after Maurice-Denis's *La petite fille à la robe rouge*

The girl in the red dress
is coming apart. Nothing
is holding her together
but imagination.
She's hurrying, but it's too late.
The gun has just gone off,
the water has already risen,
the car has skidded into the curve.
Once, she might have made it,
but now she knows too much
for eagerness or optimism.
Her heart is old
though her step is light.
All that remains is something
civilized: polite
consideration. So she's hurrying
out of the picture to spare us the sight
of her indifferent surrender.
She knows it will happen to us, too.
She knows we are all coming apart,
that nothing holds anyone together
but imagination, pretense,
a rare day of good weather.

Sorrow Figure

The toys are lying on the floor. They're some kind of doll, plastic and bendable, blue and green, about six inches tall. The little boy calls them his "figures" and plays with them every day, imagining family romances with complicated plots. One blue figure is always placed off to the side, standing on its feet but bent over with its hands pressed to its face. From a distance, no one can tell what separates this one from the rest of the group—whether he's an expatriate, an exile, a pariah, a leper. "Let me introduce you to the sorrow figure," the little boy said one day. "He's so sad no one can help him." It was then I noticed the sorrow figure in the sunshine, glowing, a haze of blueness rising from its bent-down body. I leaned closer. I heard its little toy wail trapped inside the plastic body. I heard the shudders, the sobs, the oaths. And I heard, too, all the other toys chattering and enjoying being played with as if nothing like this could ever happen to them.

Ethiopia

Niobe lives in the desert, too.
She spends her days bent over
like an umbrella, bent over
the little dying things
that make no noise.
Niobe's mouth is so dry
she makes no noise, either.
She cannot talk, cannot moan.
She has given up spitting
in the mouths of those she shelters
from the desert sun. No spit
is left. No water, no rice.
There is only Niobe, always
here and everywhere else,
who cannot help herself, bending over
the dying. She does not feel
like an animal, but perhaps
she is. Others who are as strong
as she do not bend
over dying children. They save
their strength. They talk
to the government men
in the trucks. They walk
away if they can. But Niobe
is different. Niobe
bends over, Niobe
bends.

Bus Ride

Niobe is very old now.
She has hardly anything left
to lose: her teeth, her eyesight
are already gone, her hair's
falling out in gray-black clumps.
All her children are dead.
So when the white man wants
to sit down, and gives her the Look,
she can't tell if it's tiredness
or strength that keeps her fixed
on the plastic seat.
                              Suddenly
everyone is very quiet.
Heat whirs in through the open windows.
Flies flick on hat brims.
Niobe's eyes are on the floor.
The driver opens the door and tells her
to get out if she won't move back.
But Niobe won't
move back. She's lived
her life. She knows
she's right. Only god can hurt
someone as much
as she's been hurt.
And they aren't god
because they're scared
of her—an old woman
who's almost crushed
with only this much left:
to lift her chin
and look them in their eyes
and shake her head
and sit there, riding
all the way to History.

49

War Photograph

A naked child is running
along the path toward us,
her arms stretched out,
her mouth open,
the world turned to trash
behind her.

She is running from the smoke
and the soldiers, from the bodies
of her mother and little sister
thrown down into a ditch,
from the blown-up bamboo hut
from the melted pots and pans.
And she is also running from the gods
who have changed the sky to fire
and puddled the earth with skin and blood.
She is running—my god—to us,
10,000 miles away,
reading the caption
beneath her picture
in a weekly magazine.
All over the country
we're feeling sorry for her
and being appalled at the war
being fought in the other world.
She keeps on running, you know,
after the shutter of the camera
clicks. She's running to us.
For how can she know,
her feet beating a path
on another continent?
How can she know
what we really are?
From the distance, we look
so terribly human.

The Fire Mystery

Niobe is the nun
this time, sitting
in a circle of terrified
people who don't want
to watch
what she's about
to do.

The priest circles her
with a can of gas
and readies the matches
and says nothing.
But she is too far away
to hear him anyway, making
her phoenix song already, waiting
for the sun's rays
to light her up.
She is in the very small place
now, committing the ultimate
solitary act. Very deep
inside the voices of the children
rise up in her
and she can hear again
their sweet songs,
feel mouths tugging
on her swollen teats.
She wants them back
again, of course, but knows
it cannot happen now. It's over.
But she can live again
if she can die.
And those who watch
can understand the mystery
the burning body sings:

Reduced to dust
and embering ashes,
the heart remains
unburnable.
Like a dependable motor
that always starts,
it will beat again
in the bodies of those
who want it to, who understand
that love and pain
grow hand in hand
and undertake the journey
anyway, wanting to be taken
where only love can go.

Ars Poetica

At last, her hands are not shaking.
Finally, her eyes are dry.
She thinks of the dead
calmly, without terror.
She thinks of paintings and history
to remind herself how small
and insignificant
her tragedies are, how bad
they might have been.

The painter's parents
died at Dachau,
and his famous picture
shows them walking away
older than they ever were,
worn-out and gray, trudging
up a hillside forever.

She likes the painting
because its story
cannot change, cannot
continue to the nocturnal round-up,
the trains of terrified families
passing through the night.
In the painting, the dead
are walking up a mountain
forever. They will not get cold
or hungry or any older.
They will not die.

She likes to imagine
the painter at his easel,
temporarily relieved
of his tragic history
and personal pain.

For a short while, he had only
a *task:* combining color
on the palette,
a *problem:* how thickly
to apply the paint.
His tragedy eventually became a picture
—a beautiful picture.
Then someone bought it from him
and took it away.

The New Niobe

It's a myth she's a rock.
She's a new woman, hard
where she was soft before
and full of a new self-knowledge.
She won't ever open up
like that again, convinced
that nothing bad could ever happen
if a girl is good and optimistic.
Now she knows:
fate flies down
whenever god feels like it
and happens like a TV show
or someone else's tragedy
published in the paper.
Then one day the tragedy
is yours, the name
is yours, the obituary
yours. The photo
in the paper
is your backyard.
The dead boy on television
your dead boy.

And then the rock comes.
And stays
sometimes forever.
The body nailed
to the bed
like childbirth
only nothing more
than pain comes forth.

But Niobe was strong.
Too much love in her to crush.
The crushing only made her
better, like coal being turned
to diamonds. Now she's a precious
jewel to us, changed from a myth
to a woman at last:

a woman sitting
on an evening lawn
who watches the water
where her baby drowned.
She recalls his face,
his round, fat feet,
the falling sound
of his morning cry
until she is spiraling down
into the gears of god's great game.
But finally she's full
of a new self-knowledge.
She recognizes the feelings
that are winding up
and knows she can't
be crushed by them. She is hard
as the hardest diamond now.
She can say, *It happened.*
He died.
I live.

Epilogue

Now in the evenings
she sits on the long lawn
sloping down to the water
and listens to the waves slapping
like hands on the gray stone wall.
The furrows where the feelings
have ground through before
are less tender now,
worn into a callus
she's grown used to wearing.
Pain is distant, forged
into an object outside herself,
a beautiful curiosity
she can hold in her hands:
A Chinese box or a jigsaw puzzle,
needling the intellect
and ignoring her feelings.

Usually, she rocks in a brown wood chair
on the dampening grass, shadows descending
from her long dark hair.
And if you cruised up that river
in a quiet boat, you could see her
as I do, the invisible scaffoldings
of strength and pain. *If Niobe had not lived*
I could not talk to you now.
I could not love
anything at all.
No one at all.

Lamplights flick on in the house behind her
and across the water the companionable, tinny clink
of a rigging rope on the metal mast
of a docked boat.
                    Soon, she will rise
and turn her back on the river that changed her world,
and on me, the life she doesn't know she's saved.
Inside the house waits the rest of her life,
what it's become, what it can be.
She is leaving now. I can barely
see her small, slight back, the shoulders
that have borne so much moving steadily
forward into yellow light. From her hands and skirts
as she walks away, gifts are falling,
glistening and trembling in the wet, dark grass.

Notes

p. ii   The epigraph is from the title poem of Adrienne Rich's *Diving Into the Wreck: Poems, 1971–1972* (New York: W. W. Norton & Company, 1973), p. 23.

p. x   The quotation is from Ovid, *Metamorphoses*, trans. Rolfe Humphries (Bloomington, Ind.: Indiana University Press, 1955), Book VI, lines 295–323, p. 439.

p. xi   The quotation is from Homer, *The Iliad*, trans. Robert Fitzgerald (Garden City, N. Y.: Doubleday, 1974), Book XXIV, lines 600–19, pp. 587–88.

p. xi   The quotation is from Dante, *Purgatorio*, trans. C. Gordon Wright (London: Methuen & Company, 1905), Canto XII, p. 93.

p. xi   The quotation is from Edith Hamilton, *Mythology* (New York: Franklin Watts, Inc., 1942), pp. 348–49.

p. xii The quotation is from Robert Graves, *The Greek Myths* (Baltimore: Penguin Editions, 1955), p. 259.

p. xii The quotation is from Barbara G. Walker, *The Woman's Encyclopedia of Myths and Secrets* (San Francisco: Harper & Row, 1983), p. 279.

p. xiv From C. G. Jung and C. K. Kerenyi, *Essays on a Science of Mythology* (New York: Bollingen, 1949), pp. 141–42. The speaker is an unidentified Ethiopian woman, ca. 1900.

p. xv   David Ignatow's remarkable poem is from his *Poems, 1934–1969* (Middletown, Conn.: Wesleyan University Press, 1970), pp. 130–31.

p. 5   "Apollo was a tolerant if not a forgiving god. His cult discouraged killing for vengeance and encouraged lawful expiation of crime for all classes of society. Apollo himself urged Orestes to kill Clytemnestra as just punishment rather than revenge. When he himself caused the deaths of the sons of Niobe (causing her perpetual grief), he allotted the years they had not lived to Nestor, husband of Niobe's daughter, Chloris." (Richard Carlyon, *A Guide to the Gods* [New York: William Morrow, 1982], p. 151.)

pp. 6–7 "Artemis was . . . responsible for the summary punishment of many minor errors on the part of other humans; a forgotten sacrifice here, a word out of place there, was enough to bring ruin on whole dynasties and lay waste entire countries." (Carlyon, p. 153.)

59

pp. 14–15 The title is an ironic reference to the beautiful but highly idealized images of *jeunes mères* Auguste Rodin created in a number of sculptures that are on display at the Rodin Musée in Paris.

p. 46 The painting to which the poem refers is by the nineteenth-century French painter, Maurice-Denis: *La petite fille à la robe rouge,* 1899. The technique is a kind of hyperbolized pointillism: figure and landscape are composed of large, irregular dots of paint that appear to be decomposing before one's eyes.

p. 49 Rosa Parks's historic ride actually took place in cooler weather on December 1, 1955.

pp. 53–54 The painting to which the poem obliquely refers is Henry Koerner's *My Parents,* 1946–1947. Koerner's parents did die in a concentration camp during World War II; although I have said in the poem that it was Dachau, I do not know this to be the exact camp where the deaths occurred.

About the Author

Kate Daniels was born in Richmond, Virginia, in 1953. She studied English Literature at the University of Virginia, where she earned a B.A. and M.A., and writing at Columbia University, where she received her M.F.A. Her first book of poems, *The White Wave*, won the 1983 Agnes Lynch Starrett Poetry Prize. She is co-editor of *Poetry East*, and lives in Baton Rouge, Louisiana, where she teaches in the writing program at Louisiana State University.

PITT POETRY SERIES
Ed Ochester, General Editor

Archibald MacLeish, *The Great American Fourth of July Parade*
Peter Meinke, *Night Watch on the Chesapeake*
Peter Meinke, *Trying to Surprise God*
Judith Minty, *In the Presence of Mothers*
Carol Muske, *Wyndmere*
Leonard Nathan, *Carrying On: New & Selected Poems*
Leonard Nathan, *Holding Patterns*
Kathleen Norris, *The Middle of the World*
Sharon Olds, *Satan Says*
Alicia Ostriker, *The Imaginary Lover*
Greg Pape, *Border Crossings*
James Reiss, *Express*
David Rivard, *Torque*
William Pitt Root, *Faultdancing*
Liz Rosenberg, *The Fire Music*
Richard Shelton, *Selected Poems, 1969-1981*
Peggy Shumaker, *The Circle of Totems*
Arthur Smith, *Elegy on Independence Day*
Gary Soto, *Black Hair*
Gary Soto, *The Elements of San Joaquin*
Gary Soto, *The Tale of Sunlight*
Gary Soto, *Where Sparrows Work Hard*
Tomas Tranströmer, *Windows & Stones: Selected Poems*
Chase Twichell, *Northern Spy*
Chase Twichell, *The Odds*
Leslie Ullman, *Dreams by No One's Daughter*
Constance Urdang, *Only the World*
Ronald Wallace, *People and Dog in the Sun*
Ronald Wallace, *Tunes for Bears to Dance To*
Cary Waterman, *The Salamander Migration and Other Poems*
Bruce Weigl, *A Romance*
Robley Wilson, Jr., *Kingdoms of the Ordinary*
David Wojahn, *Glassworks*
Paul Zimmer, *Family Reunion: Selected and New Poems*